In The Shadow
Of A Yellow Star

In The Shadow Of A Yellow Star

POEMS

Lowell Rubin

Copyright © 2010 by Lowell Rubin.

ISBN:	Hardcover	978-1-4500-3441-8
	Softcover	978-1-4500-3440-1

This book was printed in the United States of America.

To order additional copies of this book, contact:
Xlibris Corporation
1-888-795-4274
www.Xlibris.com
Orders@Xlibris.com
66638

Contents

Dedication

To my Parents—David and Florence Rubin
and for my sons
Noah and Gideon
and theirs,
to understand
and
especially for
Margot
who has understood
so much

Introduction

This collection of poems spans many years. When I began to write poetry more seriously, I discovered that being a Jew, albeit a secular one, somehow left its mark. These poems are testimony to the impact of a variety of experiences as a Jew, since my childhood in the late 1930's and early 1940's.

Perhaps these poems can contribute, in a small way, to a better understanding of what being Jewish, but not religious, can mean. Surely, "being Jewish" can be hard to understand, particularly to those who are not, and to some of those who are as well, since the majority of Jews are no longer "religious", as is the case, probably, with the majority of Protestants and Catholics. We are learning more about what it means to be a Muslim.

We have entered an age when these designations are nominal but do represent a degree of belief or observance, but certainly not in the sense that they once did. Today we are more likely to be swept up in our everyday involvement in the modern secular world. This involvement brings us all together and makes us all appear somehow the same.

Yet, beneath the surface similarities, there lurk remnants of different pasts and different experiences that are part of different cultural traditions that sometimes can enlighten and other times, unfortunately, divide us.

So here are some shards from my own archeology.

Lowell Rubin

SUMMER OF 1989

I will try to explain.
That summer was about something different.
All summer long we were on trains
going east.

You remember the rumbling of the train cars
in the movie SHOAH,
the relentless clicking of the rails,
hour after hour, that journey ...
to the end of the world.

We boarded the train in Amsterdam
after climbing the stairs
to see where Anne Frank's family
tried to hide.
We were on our way back to Berlin.
The Wall was still there,
that spiritual rent
in the soul of a people
who never quite saw it that way.

That summer Berlin was like Hades.
but there was disagreement about
.which way to Hell.
I finally understood.
Hades is crowded, mysterious, full of intrigue,
an air of tension hanging over it.

We walked through the Tiergarten on Sunday
after an outdoor piano concert.
The park was filled with old men in wheel chairs,
or hobbling on crutches, leaning
on their upright wives in 1930's dresses.
It was such a peaceful scene.

Why do I still have trouble going to Germany
and trouble not going to Germany.
Why do I think about how old everyone is
who I am talking to.
Why did we go to Germany that summer
and continue eastward.
We had explanations for it.

We wanted to see Old Europe.
We wanted to see what was not destroyed.
We wanted to see what was destroyed.

We rode on to the outer rim
of the Austro-Hungarian Empire
where it was still possible to use German
with a few of the old people,
to Prague and Budapest and then Cracow.

The Jews were sent far away.
No one should see this barbarism.
No one should know where it came from.

As the train rumbled on, walls were falling.
all over Eastern Europe.
It was a strange summer.
In one month
we made our way through the 20th Century.

Czechoslovakia was as tight as a drum.
You felt faint, the atmosphere was so thick,
about to explode.
We telephoned Jiri. We could never reach him.
Our Franz Kafka, in the guise of a mechanical
engineer, who worked in a clock factory,
whom me met our first time in Prague.

In the end we didn't go to the beautiful,
contorted, Art Deco restaurant that night.
You couldn't face it.
Instead we had an expensive dinner wheeled to our room.
Champagne, Filet Mignon, white table cloth and silver.
We needed to escape.
Several times that summer, when it was too much,
we let ourselves be "rich" Americans,
as when, we finally flew out of Warsaw, in desperation,
on Swiss Air, back to Budapest,
where we had left some luggage.

We had not meant it to be that way.
The first time we boarded the train to leave Poland
our new found Polish friends from the art gallery
told us, push, don't worry. This isn't civilization anymore.

At the Czech border, other Poles and some Czechs whom
we had met on the train translated to the passport control.
Your mother was dying, we had to get back.
But they wouldn't listen.
They threw us off the train
in the middle of the night
at the border.
They would not let us through Czechoslovakia
with all our visas, so painstakingly obtained.

Was it the conversation in our hotel room
a week before in Prague?
Igor, the other young Czech we met, was fearless
in his conversation, even though we knew,
the room might be bugged.
Did someone see me slip him
a volume of Winnicott
in the lobby of the Hotel InterContinental,
to bring to his girlfriend who was studying psychology.

Being American can protect you only so much.
That was one of the things we learned that summer
on the ride back to Cracow from the Czech border,
sitting in the aisle on upturned plastic milk racks
that the trainman let us use as seats,
for two American dollars.
We huddled together in the madness
that came with each stop,
people rushing in and down the aisles
trying to sell anything, the shirt off their back,
even old plastic bags.

We played dumb in every language that we knew
threw up our hands.
But even with all that desperation,
somehow, now it was different.
We had been to Auschwitz.

It is a simple trip from Cracow.
A taxi will take you there.
The camp was divided into two parts,
you remember.
Birkenau, where the ramps are.
In the surrounding fields a farmer was haying.
You see the long simple buildings
which stand like decaying barns,
a trench down the middle, the wooden racks
at the sides.

I lay down for a moment
on the wooden planks.
I remembered how it felt months later
when I awoke from my sleep, naked,
shivering, freezing from the terrible cold.

The other part of the camp, Auschwitz,
one desolate brick building after the other
and here and there the ovens.
We descended into the changing rooms,
the. "showers".

Why were we there, why had we come.
"A strange way to celebrate your 25th Wedding
Anniversary," our children said. "Why not Italy . . .
you know".

I remember the people of Budapest lining the banks
of the Danube, singing as the fireworks went off
to at last celebrate freedom, on that St. Stephen's Eve,
as we watched from the balcony of the Hotel Gelert.
One long ordeal was over.
It was happening everywhere, gradually, and then
in a torrent.
I kept wondering.
What did we come to witness?
Why were we there.

Then I realized, I was a survivor,
more than I knew.
Though only a child,
during a war far away,
something was burned into my flesh. I could remember,
names they had called me
"Kike", "Yid".

Now I knew why
we had to go together,
to make that journey into Death . . .
and come back.

WEDDING POEM

Buenos Aires to Hartford,
a long journey
not without tears, even if
in their final shedding, joyful.

Traveling between languages.
In the end not such a long way,
if they are joined by the language
of the heart.

How far was it between the Ukraine,
North and South America, even South Africa.
You had the same Russian grandfathers and grandmothers,
all wanderers. Jews have that curse and that blessing.
They make their El Dorados in Argentina
or Hartford.

When you go up the Rio de la Plata,
can you see Buenos Aires, as we see Hartford
from the Connecticut river.

Hartford had a poet, Wallace Stevens,
who understood it well, those journeys to far off places,
although his other language was French.
He wore business suits, thought about insurance
most of the day, but wrote poetry
early in the morning.

He wrote about strange birds,
the way words conjure thought,
and the meditative moments of a life.

You never know where the music hides,
or photographs of glory are put away.
He would have been among the first to say
Hartford, or Rosario, Cardoba, Catamarca,
Salta, or Springfield, they are not so far apart.

It is sometimes at night, or early in the morning,
that you remember and shake yourself.
Is this where I am and where
I will be tomorrow.
But you grow roots in the heart of another
and find a place where the wandering ceases.
A woman is settling, connecting, rooting.
A soil to sow.
A man drives horses, pulls ploughs,
sometimes with his teeth, if he has to.

So now the streams flow together,
the Plata and the Connecticut,
gathered up, on their way to the ocean.

Water bore us, water covers us,
water connects us.

It will bless you as the streams flow,
one into the other
making dreams come true.

THE SABBATH QUEEN

She cloaks her head and gestures.
Come to me spirit of the Holy One.
She prays the familiar words,
the woman's prayer ...
Come spirit of the Sabbath and fill this house.
Bless us all.
She gestures yet again. Come forth.
Then lights the candles and folds her
hands across her eyes, repeats
the incantation that unites this tribe.
Lord of the Sabbath come in.
Make our home your home.
Her hands still shade her eyes,
not to see the brightness.
And He enters, as the wind, and
makes the candles flicker.
The Sabbath has begun.

THE JEWISH HOLIDAYS

(a Talmudic argument)

Every year we would have a different celebration.
Don't you remember.
Some years we would go to the movies with the children
for Chanukah.
Remember the one about the Rabbi who had a car
that flew.

> *Every year I want to do the same thing.*
> *So the words should be the same.*
> *That way I get to know them.*
> *I will remember them, know*
> *how they go.*

Every year it had to be different.
Some years we would look at the Haggadah
by Ben Shahn, other years by Baskin.
Or, that New Year, do you remember
when I took you to hear
Shlomo Carlsbach, the singing Rabbi.

> *It should never vary, otherwise it is so*
> *confusing.*
> *Not just confusing, but how can you enjoy it.*
> *What is to enjoy is how it goes over and over*
> *until you hear it in your mind and find*
> *your mouth saying the words.*

So every year we would revise, change the words,
the pictures, make the story of Purim a little different.
How can you keep it alive. Otherwise
it would seem dead to me.
I had to re-write every holiday.
I did it myself. Even though, what do I know?
I looked. I thought about it. For me that was good enough.
It keeps your mind alive, wakes up your heart.

>*It doesn't have to be the same people.*
>*There can be new people.*
>*But everything else has to be the same.*
>*The same prayer book, the same reading.*
>*How can it be other than that it is the same.*
>*Can you tell me? No.*
>*So that doesn't matter to you.*
>*That's what I thought!*

Every year for us it was a different dance, a different wine.
Don't you remember. We never took a vacation
in the same place: new sights, new vistas,
.that is what life is about.

If you really believe, it is wonderful to hear
the same story over and over, to know it is still
there
to be reassured.
Otherwise, what is important gets lost.
I wouldn't enjoy it.
That is how it should be. What gives peace.

How could I stand it if it was always the same.
You have to let your imagination go. Let it soar.
Upwards, Downwards. Wherever it needs to go.
That will guide you.
Every New Year should really be new.
Every Passover different.

ON THE IDEA
OF THE HOLY ONE

How could the sought after God
have ever created life.
What God could bear the weight
of this creation.
The torture and death.
The infinite agonies of restless being.
The chaos. The struggle to stand desire.
Where do we find praise,
for the murderer, the torturer,
the blind God,
creator of life.

SHOFAR

Through the gnarled horn,
a bleeting,
a cry... a beseeching.

The sound that divides the years,
cutting the old
from the new.

It is a sound meant
to wake you up,
and freeze your heart.

The sound of
over five thousand years
of triumph and sorrow.

That is how God speaks,
with thunder and lightening,
with bushes on fire.

Through the horn
of a beast.
Praise the Lord.

The sound is eerie,
the screech of an animal
about to be slaughtered.

The sound of
frightened children
about to die.

It is strange ... unexpected,
these are solemn days
filled with lamentation.

It is after all a death
as well as
a beginning.

It is that death that
prepares us for death.
Days that tell us
that
our days
are numbered.

So it is proper
to go to a corner and read,
to look out of the window,
to meditate.

It is proper to wonder
what is proper?
What is it you should do?

Even if it defies the Lord God.
Even if that
is what you have to do.

The Jewish New Year is somber
the sun of the New Year
has yet to shine.

It is a pious time
a holy time.

The time to
beg for forgiveness
is almost upon us.

Your lips are moist with honey.

I will cover them
with my prayers of hope.

PRAISE THE LORD FOR IRVING GINSBURG

Irving Ginsburg,
why am I thinking of you.
God only knows.

Friend of my father's young manhood
What do I know of you.
What do I remember.

He always spoke of your long walks together
discussing Marx and Freud.

You were not a hero to many,
unmarried, childless,
a provincial Jewish lawyer,
beloved uncle of a Yale Law Professor,
your claim to fame.
(I remember how proud you were
that your nephew, Professor Goldstein,
was a protégé of Harold Laski.)

And who remembers Laski now.
Doesn't anybody study history,
recall England between the wars,
remember the conscience of the Labor Party,
the visiting Harvard Professor
who was on the ramparts during
Boston's great policeman strike.

What happens to those lessons
from the past,
all our mistakes.
I'm sure Irving Ginsburg could
have helped us, despite
his lack of celebrity.

But he died in the Jewish Home for the Aged
in Springfield Massachusetts.

No one would have recognized him
with his mouth gaping open,
staring into space.
Yet... it was amazing.
More than sixty years after
their long walks together,
my ninety year old father
made a pilgrimage,
saw what was left of his old friend Irving,
sitting there, with someone stuffing
food into his mouth.
And Irving's eyes lit up.
God how was it.

Old and long deaf.
No visit announced or expected.
This man, unable to speak,
looks up at my father for a long time,
then his eyes light up.
Sounds focus on his lips

De ... Deh ... Da ... Dah ... Dav ... Dave ... David

So Praise the Lord
for this heart,
for this crazy mind we have,
for friendship.
Praise the Lord
for Irving Ginsburg.

LINE BREAK
FOR THE NEW YEAR

Rosh Ha Shonah, the New Year, is just
the continuation of the old year,
with a line break
at the end.
You can feel the en-
jambment,
in the way your life moves to
the next line, before the year is
done.
That is why you need
a horn... to sound.
Better if it is strange and
haunting.
So hear the ram's horn, the Shofar
blow.
Ah, Ah, Ah, Ah
Ow...
It is time. The old year is
over and you shall be inscribed
on the Day of Atonement in
the book of life, forgiven,
if you are penitent,
for all your sins
of the old year.
Only their echo remains
Shonah Tovah.

BAT MITZVAH

A Rabbi,
wrapped in a Prayer Shawl,
wrapped in a memory,
with a guitar,
takes us from the week
to the Sabbath.
Sing with me
a song without words
without time.

Bim bam
Bim bim bim bam
Bim bim bim bim bim bam

A child/woman
follows her mother,
with her mother' smile.
A woman/child.
A woman still a child,
who will make a child,
who will bring
a family into the world.

I look at the faces
of these young women
in a row of friends, young girls.
They giggle and laugh, they
wriggle and touch their soft,
unformed bodies, in a knowing way
... and what do they know!

My mother told me
that she and her friend Mildred
when they left the house
in the morning to go to school,
when she lived in Brooklyn,
where she moved from Avenue A
on the lower East Side...

She told her teacher,
"we are moving to the country".
When they were two blocks away
from the house,
they took off their midi smocks,
to reveal low cut blouses.
They read poetry
and dreamed of
men with mustaches,
like my father.

Feelings, where do they come from.
At first, you don't quite know,
from where or when.
All of a sudden
from nowhere,
you find a tear.
Sounds become places,
become pictures.
You see her face,
feel her arms around you.

Bim bam

My Yiddisha mama,
a little girl born in the new world,
her Roumanian parents,
their dry goods store,
the hours of work.
My mother who dreams,
looks at paintings,
listens to classical music.

The sounds of two worlds
The old and the new.

Bim bim bim bam

As I watch this young woman
hold the Torah
feel the weight of it
and her tradition.
I know she will pass on
more than she knows,
more than she can realize.

Bim bam
Bim bim bim bim bim bam

ANGELS

Lord, I struggle with Angels
not just devils.
What else would you have me do.
Their bodies are golden.
Their wings spread to heaven
like white sails.
Oh, Celestial Navigator
you know the currents of air.
But for the rest of us
it is all darkness.
No Holy light.

As a dying man
let me remember the struggle
in the darkness, the fumbling
of bodies.
She was beautiful even when
my heart was broken.
We lost our way.
I was no wrestler.
I had to learn the holds.
You did not tell me
how the angels would appear,
the forms they would take:
creatures neither god nor human.

There were no instructions.
Just wrestle with them.
So here I am Lord.
I have been wrestling through
the long nights, sometimes
there is only blackness.
No one tells me if you, or
even they, are there.
Just carry on and have faith
you said, something will
come of it.
Perhaps, I will learn my strength,
or hers.
I don't even remember
that you told me
it was alright to wrestle
with a woman, if she should
turn out to be an angel.
Perhaps, you even forbade me.
Was there another Commandment.
But angels, they feel like women,
but, they fight like men.

You didn't tell me.
Am I supposed to win.
It's all a mystery, Lord.
So here I am.
At the white light
of another day.
And the angel is
flying upward, returning
to you.
If she comes back
at the end of day, will I
have the strength Lord,
to wrestle once again.
According to your commandments
I am your servant.
But somehow
the angel's golden body
haunts me and I am
hers Lord, through
another night.

THOMAS WOLFE AND ALINE BERNSTEIN

You will write your heart out.
You will travel until you have to come back,
until everything aches and nothing you see
means anything anymore.
You will long for her, so unlike you.
A country boy who got lost in a library.
She spending half her life
in the Algonquin, after theater.

How will you find her.
Will she care,
even after you have abused her
in some ugly, drunken, self hating mood.

Somehow, she will be there
loving you. Waiting. While you wander
on that great search for knowledge
of the heart of the world.

She takes you back
after all the disappointments.
She cradles you in her arms,
you, almost twice her size.
Perhaps she knows that in your
poetic prose, you
are the true heir of Whitman.

Oh, you could be a monster,
a dumb giant, an oaf with an axe,
to her sequined sensibility.
Her shiny dress, a light
in the midst of darkness,
a great white way for your landing,
with your spent heart and restless mind.

And where will she find you now.
Somewhere fallen in an alley, or
holed up in a small room,
surrounded by stacks of typewritten pages
that couldn't fit into a book.

That was the trouble.
That's what Maxwell Perkins said.
Such a talent. Such a waste.
He kept whittling you down.
You just kept writing, pouring it out,
wild as an overrun mountain stream.
So where did it end.
Did you just disappear.

Come back Tom. It's alright.
She is here.
You can come home again.

A TERRIBLE DIN IN THE HOUSE OF THE LORD

In the house of the Lord
there was a great roar,
like the clatter of pans
falling out of every closet
in the Universe.

A sound not of the makers
making but of those
who would destroy everything
in their father's house.

And you may ask
why does the Almighty not
discipline them.
Take them in hand.

But the sad fact is
that the Almighty fell asleep
after the great labors of creation,
and has not yet awoken, even
with the terrible crash
and unholy shaking
that has taken place
since.

DARK ANGELS

I know about Dark Angels.
I have seen a few.
When you have lost hope
they appear. Shadowy presences,
with only a word or two.
They touch your hand or wrist.
Perhaps your lips, or gently brush
against your shoulder.
It is not warmth they give, but fear.
When you think your supply
of hope has run out,
they come with an evil smile.
Malevolence, it is said.
Just what they are up to.
Why they are there.
That is a mystery they do not share.
Whatever you are doing they say,
"let us come and help you,
we will negotiate the price
some other time," an old story.
They do not wrestle. They abide.
Those dark angels just inside.

ON THE COAST OF BOHEMIA

You are standing on an ocean beach.
The waves wash up on your ankles.
You are not concerned, it is just a little cold.

The beach is on the coast of Bohemia
where there is no coast.
The place is completely landlocked,
except that it is Shakespeare's Winter's Tale
and you have run away.

You had to run away, or be killed.
In that way it is just like the Bohemia
we know, where everyone was killed
if they were Jews or Gypsies.

And now the waves have come in,
in force.
You feel the undertow, but
you are still standing.
They didn't kill you.
You realize it's a miracle.

But you aren't ready to praise God
for the miracle.
You are not sure which God it would be
or, even exactly where you are,
or who you are. All the
information necessary if you are going
to praise God... so you don't.
Maybe that's safe. Maybe not.

Why isn't everything clearer
and more certain, you ask.
But then, what do you expect
if you are half submerged in water
on the coast of Bohemia.

SUN SWALLOWER

The joke was ...
whatever ailed you,
my mother's uncle,
Max Rosenblum,
had a cure.

You go outside
on a sunny day.
You sit in a deck chair,
open your mouth,
and let the sun's
God given rays,
do their healing work.
Otherwise, he was not
a religious man.

Think of the long history
of sun worshipers,
the Egyptians or the Incas,
who wore shimmering
costumes of gold,
who held aloft long poles
topped by round glowing disks
as in their thousands they marched
to show their god-like power.

To no avail. Think of all the dead,
left behind by the Conquistadors,
driven by their lust for treasure.
The old desire to see
the fabled streets of gold.
An image that drives men mad,
and makes them willing to kill
and die to this day.

Uncle Max was not a greedy man.
He made cigar boxes and primitive
paintings in his spare time.
An immigrant, he didn't get confused.
He only had known streets that ran
with blood not gold.

Did he come to conquer.
Who would he have killed.
Don't be foolish.
Of course, he had his dreams.
But his idea was to make a living
and not be killed.

Did it ever occur to him to swallow
the sun. He would have thought
the idea mad. Madder than
he seemed to some.
What was it that he was seeking,
open mouthed. Some thought...
beware of flies.

He was not the conquering kind.
Except in love. More like
the kind who died at
the conquerer's hand.
Only a few years separated him
from the gas chamber,
come to think of it.
It was only a modest cure he sought.

THE MIND OF GOD

In every war and conflagration
they lie
in various positions of repose,
enemy
and friend.
Their guts spilled.
The ground "hallowed" by their blood.

In the sky fire.
In their eyes darkness.
In God's mind
Nothing.

PREPARING FOR PASSOVER

A little girl asks
so many questions-
not just four.
She asks about
the blue
of the sky
the green
of the grass.
Why the clouds
go by.
She asks about
the names
of the trees
the color
of bees.

Sometimes it seems
that all
she is made of ...
is questions.

Her mother and father
who have grown tall,
have questions, too,
they no longer ask.

So the little girl
helps them,
helps them to
ask those questions
once again.

But they
are not supposed to
ask questions.
Only have
the answers.

Why is the subway
noisy
and the park
so big,
the elevator
so full
of people.

Why is that man
wearing a
blue and white cloth
over his head
and shoulders.

Those who have
grown tall
try to answer
and remember.

So why is
this night different
from
all other nights.

Because we are
all together
and repeating.
Because we are
telling
part of
our story.
Because
some of those
we love
are not here.

And why
do we eat
special foods.
Because
our parents
ate these foods
and we try
to remember,
try to know
what they knew,
and maybe
what they
never knew.

So ask
the questions
children
and together
we will try
to find
answers.

THE SUN

The sun, even in winter,
enters the window through
the blinds, its light touching
and warming everything in its
reach.

I feel the warmth, even of
its lengthened rays, and see
the dance of life that it sustains
in the flickering light show
against the wall.

We will always be sun worshipers
and infidels no matter what,
until our death, when the sun
will no longer warm us.

That is the Golden Calf.
We praise it and seek it
despite all other gods,
here, where we are so perilously
poised on the edge between
burning up and freezing.

Like a warm shower we
do not want to leave,
the sun holds us.
Every day we are in its grace.
Its absence, misery,
its presence,
the staff of life.

What flower would bloom.
What morsel to eat without
its indulgence.
So I am transfixed looking at
this light on my wall.

I did not make it, nor do I know
how it came to be.
It is sufficient that it is.

HEINE

"I am a German poet
In German lands I'm famed
When the proudest names are mentioned
Then mine is also named

And, child, the thing that hurts me
Hurts many a German breast
When the worst of griefs are mentioned
Mine are among the rest

                           Heinrich Heine from,
                      Wenn ich an deinem Hause

We were talking about Heinrich Heine.
We were talking about suffering,
about mad poets. Hölderlin in fact.
And you said, "Heine was in terrible pain
in his last years. They had to carry him around.
his body was so twisted".

Heine, the Jewish Poet, from Dusseldorf

So now when all the German Jews
have been hobbled, even those
who did stand tall,
some good citizens of Dusseldorf decided to
honor "their great poet".

One suggestion was that they name
the local university after him.
After all, he was a good German, and even a
convert to Christianity,
however haunted by his Jewish memories.

But there was an uproar...
Name a university after a Jew.
Let them do that in Israel, or even America. *

So what to do to honor "their" famous son,
to salve their bad conscience.
They decided to put up a statue.
Well, they knew a perfect sculptor,
a former Nazi.

How did it come out you want to know.

There in a park in Dusseldorf is just a head,
large enough so that children can climb over it:
the face thrown back
looking up, with
a terrifying large beaked nose,
like a bird,
to let all the world know
that this Heinrich Heine was a Jew
born in Dusseldorf,
also a poet.

Post Script

* In 1999, after this poem was written, the Rectors of the University in Dusseldorf reversed their earlier decision and renamed the University in Dusseldorf, the Heinrich Heine University.

WITTGENSTEIN

The Tractatus

You can hear his voice
with its shushing accent,
that soft Viennese German.
But he was not soft.

He was so sure of himself.
They said his mind
was like the steel
that made his family rich.
Critics beware.
Remember when he later brandished
a fireplace poker
in an informal debate with Karl Popper.

At age 22, in the midst of the 1st World War
inside a trench, he scribbled down his
ideas about philosophy, influenced
by Spinoza, Schopenhauer and Bertrand Russell.
He was obsessed.

He was certain that he
was the discoverer
of new truth,
as only a brilliant
young man can be.

After all, one of the greatest
Cambridge philosophers, G.E. Moore,
was sent to take dictation from him
in a prisoner of war camp.

These scribbling were later
to become the basis of
his undergraduate thesis at Cambridge,
his *Tractatus.*

He was to turn philosophy
on its head, until he turned
his back on his own creation.

The rule was
no one could speak.
except him. No one could
define or describe,
except him, the
genius son
of a millionaire.

He spoke like
the Lord of Creation.
He separated the land from the sea.
He gave everything its name and place.

He begins with a quotation "... and whatever
a man knows, whatever is not mere rumbling
and roaring that he has heard,
can be said in three words ".

And then he began again.
Summing up his little book,
"what can be said at all
can be said clearly,
and what we cannot talk about
we must pass over in silence".

The right word was as important
to the philosopher as it is to the poet.
He was certain that he was not a poet. And yet,
after all his efforts, one reviewer wrote
of the whole *Tractatus*, that it was a poem.

How can someone who is trying
to be so exacting be translated. It
is worse than trying to translate poetry.

He begins in his logical way
with a 1.0 and then 1.1, then 1.11
then 1.2 followed by 1.21 and then 2
Now what is logical or mathematical
about that. Where was 1.3 and so on.

So you see why some people think he
was writing a poem. But he was
a dictator. Things were as he said
they were. Didn't the mathematician
Charles Dodgson, whose pseudonym was Lewis Carrol,
have the Queen say in *Alice,*
"Words mean whatever I say
they mean".

Wittgenstein's point was that
certain things could be talked about
and other things could not be talked about.
What could be talked about was precise
but abstract. Logical propositions.
What could not be talked about
was anything psychological.
He was very distrustful of Freud.

But maybe what could not
be talked about was
what needed to be talked about.
Such as his being Jewish by backround,
in a non Jewish world. Or, his being
homosexual, which he
could not accept in himself.

He would say these things
were not worth talking about
because they were unsolvable.

But what could not be said,
followed him and haunted him.
They followed him to the coast
of Norway where he had gone
with a male companion.

Those things that could not be
talked about, remained. Until
someone talked about them
long after, when it no longer
would do him any good. But he
was not about to let anyone
tamper with his mind.

No question he was brilliant.
Mathematician, Philosopher, Engineer.
He designed an extraordinary house
for his sister, for diversion.
And he dazzled those who listened.

Wherever he went they followed him,
until he left them,
and went off on a different path.
Some of the ideas he spun out
remain. But so do the things
that he would not talk about.

HEIDEGGER AND HANNAH

She was a beautiful young Jewess.
He was Herr Professor. It was 1924.
He showed great interest.
He encouraged her.
You know the rest of the story.

But it was not so simple.
He was married. Not unusual.
How could she know that he would be
more of a traitor to her cause, and his own,
than she could even suspect.

His great teacher was a Jew. Husserl.
At the beginning Heidegger was still
visiting his old Professor, journeying
to see him.
He mentioned this to her.

But that was not what was really
on his mind. It was about Being,
he said. He was avuncular.
"The path your young life will take is hidden".
But there was urgency in his voice:
"Dear Miss Arendt!...
I must come to see you this evening
and speak to your heart... We never know
what we can become for others
through our Being".

Surely, something was consummated then,
more than a pure meeting of minds.
Something that kept her attached to him
beyond Being and Time, beyond Reason.

Their paths would eventually separate
but never entirely part. Through the most dismal
of times, through utter catastrophe that flung
her across an ocean and a world away from him,
she did not give up. "Martin ..." she wrote
from time to time over the next forty years.

It has been said that he was the greatest philosopher
of the 20th Century, and she was to become
its conscience. His subject was Being, back to Plato,
back to nearly the beginning of Philosophy
But in the end did she know
more about Being than he.
Being not just in the head
but in the world.

KINGDOM COME

So who are you I asked,
"Death", he replied, "You
have stumbled into my valley".
Show me where
the exit is, I said.
"Which one," he replied,
with a smile.

I was on a line in Auschwitz.
Which line should it be.
Which was the way to the shower.
It has been so long since I was clean.

The bells were ringing.
Am I out of my mind. Almost.
I am reassured.
You are here with me,
between sleep and waking,
between night and day.
In the hour of death.

But time is suspended.

He said," I take it back, you will
have five more years, no ten,
perhaps twenty".

I can't remember now, exactly, what he said.

Why is the music stopping.
Why has it all stopped with a screech.
Was I hit by a car.
Am I lying on a battlefield
near Troy
with a spear through my abdomen
is anything leaking.
Do I seem alive to you.

Hurry,
call the surgeon,
Shahinian.
He will know how to repair this wound.
After all he stitches what remains
back to life.

So we lay on the battlefield.
There were hundreds of us
with gashes in our bellies.

All the while
the bells were ringing.
Our eyes were fogged over.
Then they came
one after the other.
These women.
They held our wrists,
looked straight ahead,
saw the marking of time,
told us not to worry,
not give up, to hold on,
to come back.
Follow their eyes into
the darkness. They would
lead us. They have
been in this valley before.

All the while
the bells were ringing
in my head.
What time is it.
Answer the telephone.
Can't you hear
it ring.

Tell me where you are.
I know this is night.
Of that I am certain.
How do I get out of here.

I kept saying
does this end.
The music,
the bells,
ringing in my ears.
Stop it.

No, let it ring on.
Which way is out ?
No, the lights.
Keep the lights on.
The bells,
who do they toll for.

I am not an English poet.
Or a Greek one.
Just a wandering Jew
who stumbled into
the valley of death
and stumbled out.

with surgeon and nurses,
with a loving wife and children,
without a tombstone,
with bells and yes,
a jagged wound.

The bells are still ringing.

FUNERAL IN LOS ANGELES

Why must it be
that as they file past us,
the family of mourners,
     the Jewish men and women
     of Los Angeles,
     some older, some younger,

why is it that I see the dead,
the Jewish dead of
a hundred European cities,
     love in their eyes, in their faces
     as they kiss you and
     then touch the wooden casket.

Why do I see the dead
come back to life.
     Whose life do we mourn,
     which dead.
This is how the dead are
still alive and we become
their witness.

Is that our fate as
Jews at the end of the 20th Century
at every holiday, at every Bar Mitzvah
at every funeral to
have to see the dead
come back to life.
> They hover over us,
> marching endlessly in procession,
> marching to the gas chamber,
> cold concrete walls,
> a door closing.

When did they smell
that horrible sweet smell of death.
What did they say
at the end.
Haven't you always wondered.
Whom did they embrace
among strangers.

I wish I could get over it.
The living should not be dead.
The dead should not be living.
This century has got us
all mixed up.

Must we who are living
carry the burden of the dead.
Are we sent to correct God's mistakes.
Is that it. A God who sends his
children to correct his mistakes.
Is that possible.

Before the time is up
give me your questions.
Only the questions.

It is not the son
who doesn't know the answers,
who is the ignorant one.
Let those among the living
with all the answers
have some humility.

So it is to the dead we come
at the hour of mourning.
What is a good life?
What are we here to do?
What is important.

I listen at every funeral
to learn the answers.

THE REMEMBRANCE . . .

"Die Erinnerung"

She brought out a silver case.
On it was inscribed, "Die Erinnerung".
She said later that it was a cigarette case
that his father gave him, probably for a birthday.

He is gone now. They were childless.
We remember him so well.
The way he looked: thin, of medium height,
graceful, proud... so mannerly.

Slowly you opened the silver case.
In it were two triangles of yellow felt sewn together.
I would never have imagined.
Six points. Small, with a little safety pin.

She was about to move.
In a mood of giving away.
She said it was not planned.
She gave it to me.

I held his Yellow Star in my hand.

In my old age I had become
a son of history.

I AM THEIR MEMORY

I cannot help it.
European Jewry
is in my bones.
Those who vanished,
they were reborn in me.
I will not let them go.
So make bridges to
whatever century you like,
mine go backwards.

I am letting them pass,
slip over, one by one.
The line is long.
They have waited patiently.
I will not let them down.

They were not all poor.
In my eyes
the women are dressed
in their furs, cloche hats,
matched pearls around their necks,
setting off beautiful black,
silk, handmade dresses.

I stand with the gentlemen,
a hand me down pocket watch in hand.
In summer, a single piece bathing suit.
In winter, a long, fur lined
overcoat, with a sable collar.

I have stolen back the clothes
taken from them,
read the books that were burned,
and before I die,
my sons will inherit it all:
all the memories of mountains and lakes,
all their loves and kisses.
So don't worry my sweet ones,
something has been saved,
even after death and disaster.

EIN YIDDLE MIT EIN FIDDLE

I am not a Yiddle
who plays the fiddle.
I only write to sing.

But I hear music.
Sometimes in the air, or
underneath the earth.

They still play music there.
I can hear them.
Under the dark earth.

Playing on forever.
Those other Yiddels
with their fiddles.

Oy! Gott in Himmel

Acknowledgements

I want to acknowledge the part that the workshop led by the poet, Alan Dugan, over many summers at the Truro Center for the Arts, had on my development as a poet. Dugan was a fierce critic who would shout gruffly, "I don't know what that means", or, "that's not a poem, just pretty words".

It took some fortitude to withstand Dugan's withering looks and blistering criticism. But in the end it was like an axe that cleared away dead branches. There would be the final reward to read aloud with Dugan at the end of the summer with the other stalwart members of that group, at the annual Dugan Poetry Workshop reading, at the Wellfleet Library.

Several of the most important members of that workshop have struggled on together with me, since Alan's death. They are Rosalind Pace, Henry Seiden and Marcia Simon. We have added, Steve Durkee, Barry Hellman, Margaret Phillips and Gail Wynne, who have all become valued colleagues.

For Dugan, for all who left the group and all who stayed, I give thanks and offer this book.

It has also been my privilege to be part of shorter workshops led by Mark Doty, Maxime Kumin, Thomas Lux, Sharon Olds, Marge Piercy, Robert Pinsky, and Alan Shapiro. My fellow poets in those workshops were dedicated, serious, and often helpful, as were our mentors.

My wife, Margot, has been an inspiration, a valued commentator, as well as editor, and my lifelong companion and love.

To all who have accompanied me along the way, I am grateful. Aspiring poets take advantage of many gatherings of friends to offer a poem or two. They have all been gracious.